BEST BARBER EVER

STORIES FROM THE CHAIR

LAKEITH JONES

Edited by Stephanie Riese
Cover photo: Angelica Guardado
Editorial and art direction: Chad Harrington (YouPublish.com)
Cover and interior design: Bryana Anderle (YouPublish.com)

To everyone in my chair, past, present, and future.
To God be the glory.
In loving memory of Melody Rendon & Morris Akers

ACKNOWLEDGMENTS

I would like to thank, primarily, my lovely wife, Stephanie Jones, for always supporting and believing in me, keeping the house and family together while I worked. You are amazing and I love you. To our children, Aidan, Avery, Joseph, and Legend, you are the reason I work hard. To my Bellus Squad at the Academy: LaLa, Chris, Jess, Reno, Ms. B, Bryson, Andrew, and Nae; my NEX Crew: Ailyn, Keisha, Gina (thanks for all the tools), Missy, Caroline, Lani, Mel, Cherly, Laura, Candy, and Lisa; and my superior cuts at Superior Cuts: Jerry, AJ, Adrian. To my guy Hector. To Ginger, Terra, Seantique, Seanna, Ladeja, Sean, Georgia, Clyde. To Will, Christen, Nick, Emily, Caleb, thanks for the roof over my head. To Andrew and Cindy, I could not have asked for better mentors. To Stephanie Riese, editor extraordinaire, you know what you did; this book would not be what it is without your help. To the gang—Jordan, Daniel, Jasmine, Jake, Kylie, Justin, Agustinus, ZB, Torin, Ryan, Hope, Hannah, Thorne, Kiah, Rosie and Brian, Aimee, Dillon, Ashley, Hunter Richard, Ceina, Ole Ben, Abigial, Heather, Josh, Brantley, Colton, Pat, Kim, Grammy Sue, —and to the guys—Al, Manny, TJ, Ojo, Corderist, Breezy. To Kendall, Sally, Kari & Thomas, the McKoys, Carlos, Jeanie & Morris, Terry & Tina, and many more—thanks for everything and love forever. And last but certainly never least, to all my clients, THANK YOU for your support, loyalty, challenges, lessons, and inspiration.

The inspiration for this book came from my interactions with incredible people. Months into my journey, I realized these stories *had* to be told. I left out so many, but hopefully that's motivation for a second edition. I do not remember who suggested a book first, but it happened. I thought about the title *Behind the Chair*, but it was Jim who suggested *Stories from the Chair*. I do not think I am the best barber ever, but more on that later. I want to thank Ben and Heather McKoy, Andrew and Cindy Stroud, Jerry Jay-Kelley, Blair Murphy, Agustinus Soegeng, Josh Vogel, Stephanie Riese, James Riley, Nehemiah Nunez, Jordan Ray, Will and Christen Frank, Aimee Holmes, Susie Gil, Jeannie Akers, Micah Fischer, Amy Flynn, Daren Mcguire, Missy Anderson and Brett and Abigail Wilson, for helping to fund this amazing project. A sizable number of my regulars were so excited for this book. My family gave me just enough inspiration every time I thought about giving up.

CONTENTS

PREFACE

Who is the greatest barber of all time? Who are the most influential barbers you can name? Ambroise Paré, Sofie Pok, Vic Blends, Vin the barber, 360 Jezzy, John Mosley, Jacob Luenbdu, the-real-trippy Christopher Perez, A.B. Moler, Mathew Andis. You must know a few of them. But how can one single individual be the best? This can become more complicated than MJ vs LeBron. The best thing about the GOAT conversation is that it IS a conversation. At the end of it, you should at least have an answer you feel is correct. The best? I have THE answer.

There is something magical about a new haircut. My friend R. Daniel had just got out of the military, and I had not seen him in years. The military had taken its toll on him, and I could tell. Walking up to greet him, I could see the anxiety radiating from him; he could barely look me in the eye. By the end of the haircut, he was a new man, and I watched his anxiety lift as the hair fell to the ground. It was truly magical. Take my brother-in-law J-town, for instance. He looks like the Lockless Monster himself before a haircut. But by the end of it, that man could be on the cover of GQ. Being someone's barber can be one of the most honorable positions. Their hair, their life, is in your hands.

If you are a great barber, you should be a part of people's great moments. Proposals, birthdays, that big interview, weddings and more. Mr. Hansen made sure I was the one cutting his hair for his wedding. It was special because his parents sat there for the entire time, which gave me a feeling that is hard to describe. I made sure not to charge him; it was a gift. I am hoping these amazing stories are a gift to you. These remarkable stories are their red-carpet moments.

INTRODUCTION

I grew up on the wrong side of Chicago, the inner city. I am the oldest of four. I never got to know my biological father, and sadly our mother passed away when we were young. My loving grandparents took us in, and I learned about kindness and hard work. We stayed with them until their time was up. My amazing auntie Ginger took the four of us in afterwards, having three kids of her own. My dad Sean used to cut my hair. Technically, my stepdad, but my dad indeed! One day, his clippers were wet, or my hair was wet, either way, it was one of the worst haircuts I received as a child. He meant well. Love you, Dad. Let's be honest, it was time to find a professional barber. From an early age, I truly admired the barber to client relationship. Especially if they got your hair exactly right. A good barbershop is truly a special place. Watch the movie *Barbershop*. My favorite barber growing up was my childhood friend Manny. He practiced on willing participants such as Al and me, and eventually, half of his football team. He got extremely good, fast. I always admired a fresh haircut or a change in someone's appearance, yet I never considered becoming a barber.

After our auntie took us in, our second-floor apartment was getting a little too cramped with all us children. I was into street life, but I truly never fit in. I finished high school with an amazingly low GPA, and my aunt told me, "You have to do something." Hanging out in my room with the PlayStation and all the food I could manage was not working. I did what every young person who does not know their next move should do . . . I joined the military. I chose one of the most storied and respected jobs in the military, a boatswain's mate. Little did I know, you did not have to score high on the ASVAB for this job. Navy special forces caught my attention, though! I had no chance at SEALs or SWCC. EOD seemed legit but I was not bright enough at that time, so it was either a diver or swimmer. I ended up choosing to become a swimmer and passed the initial test narrowly. It was on the last day of eligibility. I had a new job in the service. After all the training, we had money, something I did not really have throughout my life. I helped my family whenever I could and partied with the rest. I had to grow up in the military, but joining was the best decision I have ever made. Getting out of the military was the second-best decision I have ever made.

It proved to be harder than I anticipated. I really enjoyed going to college with the GI Bill and it was the first time in my life that I received straight A's, and I did not cheat. The Dean's List! School in California was too political! One teacher played a clip of a nighttime political TV show every day before class, never providing an explanation or reason. I received my associate's, but it was time to move on. I wanted to figure out a way to make money without a degree. My mentor at that time, Andrew, suggested barbering and thus a barber was born. I was at Bellus Academy the next week. I was starting from zero, no prior experience, and other people had already been cutting hair for years. I remember praying and saying if I do not get good at this soon, I will have to figure something else out. Eventually, things started to click and slowly but surely, I got better.

My friend Hector from college moved away to Oregon. He came back to town and wanted to reconnect over a night of beers and bowling. Our only task was to bring the ladies; he was bringing his. Unfortunately, I was fresh out of a relationship, so I was not bringing anyone. Our friend Iz brought his friend Stephanie, and we all had a fun time. While I was in the military, we bowled a lot, and I got ridiculously good at "style" bowling. For whatever reason that night, I was on fire! *I could not miss.* Ask someone who knows about my bowling tricks. I admit there was flirting going on between Stephanie and me. We exchanged contacts at the end of the night. We did it the old school way, we dated for a few months, and I asked her to be my bride. She said yes, and I inherited two lovely kiddos, Aidan and Avery. We went on to have two boys, Joseph and Legend! Our friend Matt helped us buy a home in California and this piqued my interest in the housing market. Shortly after, I became a realtor. Barbering will always have a huge piece of my heart. It would be a dream for us to open a barbershop and a bowling alley. It is okay to dream, right?

Chapter 1

RAMBO
Stories from the Chair

At the Navy Exchange, certain clients only let certain barbers cut their hair. If you are lucky enough to grab up someone's client one day, they will A) never come back to you again, B) make you their backup (there is nothing wrong with this), or C) love you and become your permanent client.

Rambo walked into the barbershop looking for his regular barber. She had done what so many barbers have done in the past—moved on without telling most of their clients. Rambo's loyalty was so strong that he asked what shop she was now at because she only cut his hair. He had checked several times, and she was nowhere to be found. I was new to this shop, but word travels fast. "Hey, I'm sorry, bro, but she doesn't work here anymore." I made no advance. He seemed disappointed and irritated, so I just gave him space. We locked our eyes for a split second, I gave a half-smile and there he went. 1K Phew said, "Even your barber knows he cannot tempt me." He was right.

After returning to his vehicle, he started the ignition. But something told him to go back. A small, still voice, as he would later describe it. He returned, to my surprise, and said, "Hey, can you cut my hair?"

"Of course," I responded. Even though I love a good challenge, I would not encourage a regular to cheat on their barber.

But once you are in the chair, it is game on. He made it clear that this was an audition and, if I passed and he could not track down his regular barber, then he would be a loyal client. I have been in this position plenty of times and words are just words until they are fulfilled. The first haircut was a success, however, and we hit it off like the word "shipmate" on the tongue of an angry chief.

ONCE YOU ARE IN THE CHAIR, IT IS GAME ON.

Rambo would continue to come to the shop and our relationship grew. One day was different. He seemed a little shaken up. I asked what was going on and he said emergency leave. For my nonmilitary readers, emergency leave is rarely a good thing. It usually means something bad happened and you needed to return home or to the place of the incident. When I asked what happened, he went on to tell me his family was involved in a suicide attempt. A young man had decided he no longer wanted to live. He went flying down the freeway, randomly picked a car to collide with, and did just that. In these moments, it is extremely hard to continue a haircut. The base I was on used commission-based work, which meant every haircut counted. You had to be quick, effective, and efficient to make money, which was important as we are a family of six. Yet, I paused. "Are your girls, okay?"

"No," he replied, "but they are both with us still. Minor injuries, but they will never be the same." God was good to this family, despite the crazy circumstances. The driver of the other vehicle did not make it. Rambo and his family reached out to them and tried their best to give them closure. The community gathered around this family and after counseling, support, and love, they are trying to continue their lives while taking absolutely nothing for granted.

Rambo let me know how essential the haircuts were to his recovery. Although he was not directly involved, he was hurting, too. The guy gets his hair cut every three weeks and each week was a chance for us to strengthen each other. One day while I was cutting his hair and we were vibing, laughing, chatting, and planning to tackle the world, you know, guy stuff, we somehow ended up talking about the idea of a barber book. He suggested the title *Stories from the Chair* and thus a title was born.

EACH WEEK WAS A CHANCE FOR US TO STRENGTHEN EACH OTHER.

Did You Know?

Did you know? The *barba* is Latin for "beard," a classic symbol of strength, wisdom, and masculinity.

Chapter 2

MASTER CHIEF
Sometimes You Just Need
to See Your Barber

Master Chief. Not the guy from *Halo 3,* but he did wear one. A few of my clients who play basketball eventually get that work from me on the basketball court. Master Chief was not one of those guys; his team cooked mine the first time we played against each other. We had good battles, but that slice of humble pie sure didn't taste good. Anyway, he was given a barber's chair from the ship. He held on to it for several years because he didn't want it to go to waste. During Covid, our barber shop had closed, so I was cutting out of my garage because people still needed/ wanted haircuts. I denied his offer to accept this chair at least four times. But he was so convincing that eventually I took it. This made cutting at home so much easier and many people were blessed by his generosity.

Not long after, Master Chief lost a sailor. Unfortunately, this happens more often than you know in the military. After the dust settled, he told his wife he was going out. When she asked where, he said, "To see my barber." Master Chief texted me to link up, not to go for a walk and/or to talk, but for a haircut. He said what he needed at that moment was a haircut from his friend.

WHAT HE NEEDED AT THAT MOMENT WAS A HAIRCUT FROM HIS FRIEND.

In marriage, communication is key. I had been working that entire day and I just returned home to the family. I am sometimes hesitant to tell my wife certain things because her first reaction is usually strong with a healthy bit of pessimism. (I can say this because she knows it is true.) But that night, she said, "I know he needs it. Cut his hair."

After our session, Master Chief and I hugged. I said, "No charge. Please." He reluctantly agreed and went home, feeling a little better, as did I. I always thought barbers had a unique place in peoples' lives, but this confirmed that theory. Who knew that the client/barber relationship could go so deep?

Chapter 3

MRS. PICKY

Opposites Attract

Every once and again, you get the husband/wife combo. Sometimes it goes well and sometimes it's a bit much. A sweet old man told me that he was not too fussy and just needed a little touch up. He did not have much hair (like I'm one to talk!). I cleaned my tools and was ready to work. An extremely sweet, very pretty, very kind old lady came in, and he said with a smile that this was his wife. I said hello and proceeded to cut his hair while we talked about everything under the sun. At the end, I spun his chair around, and he said it looked great.

Mrs. Picky interjected, saying, "A little more here, please." Usually, the first time is understandable; your eyes can't always catch everything. There is no such thing as a perfect haircut, although that should be the aim each time. My inner thought was, "this dude has *no* hair" . . . I mean just literally strands!

I continued to cut each little spot and, suddenly, this pretty old lady wasn't so cute. But we eventually reached a point of satisfaction. To my surprise, they continued to be regular clients of mine, but she kept that same energy and I had to get used to it. I ended up liking them a lot.

SUDDENLY, THIS PRETTY OLD LADY WASN'T SO CUTE.

One day, about four months later, I saw him in the store. He tried to muster up his usual smile. I asked him how everything was going. He said two words that stopped my heart— "she's gone"! As tears streamed down his face, I gave him a small hug before I had to get back to my client. Poor guy, isn't that the way of us all? I cut his hair one more time before I switched locations, and my heart was with him. I would have given an arm and a leg to have Mrs. Picky watching over our shoulders again.

?

Did You Know?

The oldest barbershop can be found in London.

Chapter 4

LITTLE BANGS
My Super Shame

I t was not often I did ladies' hair at our barbershop, but on occa-
sion I would be brave and/or a desperate lady would come
through. A mom came in with two young daughters, one about
nine and one about six. The older of the two wanted bangs, a
haircut I knew nothing about nor had performed before in my
life. But I'm not one to avoid a chal-
lenge, sometimes to my detriment.

Fast forward—it went terrible!
Like, worst case scenario! Whatever could go wrong, did go wrong. I
grabbed way too much hair when I
started and before I knew it, it was

> **I'M NOT ONE TO
> AVOID A CHALLENGE,
> SOMETIMES TO
> MY DETRIMENT.**

meme-worthy. If Adam Sandler had given me the remote, he used
in *Click*, I would have used it. She cried, her mom cried, and I
almost cried. Her little sister let me have it. This six-year-old boss
yelled at me! It felt terrible, but in a weird way, I was really proud
of her for backing up her sister. I imagined after several months
Little Bangs would recover, but I hated that I was the main char-
acter in one of the worst experiences of her life.

As fate would have it, her father somehow ended up in my
chair. I just *had* to ask about her. He confirmed she was okay, but
also said she was scarred for several months. As you can imagine,

his haircut was free. I offered to cut his hair for free for the rest of his life, but he laughed and turned down my offer. I still regretted the whole thing, but I took solace in his haircut. Grade A.

Chapter 5

LITTLE BANGS PART TWO
My Redemption

We currently have one daughter, and her name is Avery. One summer, she wanted bangs more than anything else. Do you remember how the last one went? As a last-ditch effort, I let her know that I was willing to take her to get them done professionally. She said, "I want you to do it." Here goes nothing! I assured her that despite my terrible performance on my last attempt at cutting bangs, this one would be different. It would be like the 2007 New England Patriots getting a do-over versus the New York Giants. They would have done everything in their power to play a perfect game, and that would be my goal for my baby girl.

I watched countless YouTube videos to perfect this method. But visual learning versus putting it to the test is completely different. To her credit, she was not nervous at all. Children are so innocent that they can love unconditionally and trust. I was hoping this wasn't to her detriment. I decided I wanted this memory to last, so I filmed as many moments during this haircut as I could. This would prove to be an excellent decision.

Here goes, my first cut of bangs since my last horrendous attempt. My first trim—slow, subtle, gentle, yet with confidence. No room for mistakes! We had so much fun trimming her bangs.

Although at times she was nervous, she really liked the outcome. For some strange reason, when she realized everything was good, she went into a laughing fit. And I do not mean like thirty seconds long; I'm talking fifteen minutes straight of hysterical laughing. It was priceless. And I captured it on video. Maybe if I hadn't experienced the pain of Little Bangs, the joy of cutting my own daughter wouldn't have impacted me as much. It did.

ALTHOUGH AT TIMES SHE WAS NERVOUS, SHE REALLY LIKED THE OUTCOME.

Thank you, Avery, for trusting me to cut your bangs, which I cut again and again.

Chapter 6

CD

The Windy City

A haircut can be a time for someone to relax and get whatever they need off their chest, and although I can keep the conversation rolling, they usually carry the conversation most of the time. This was never the case with CD. He was from Chicago, my hometown, and to this day, he remains one of my only clients from back home. (As J-Man would say.)

He had a unique way of getting me to share a whole lot. I cannot explain why it's so easy for me to open up to him, but it is. (I was just texting him as I was working on this entry of the book.) CD was a dreamer! Always talking about his next move and planning the next big thing. But unlike most of us who do this, he usually followed through. CD had served as a boatswain's mate during his time in the Navy. Eventually he climbed the ranks and became a warrant officer. He probably could have kept going, but some people were bigger than the service and he was. Most people say they serve their country by joining something that's bigger than themselves and, while that can be true, it can also limit certain individuals. I wish I could share everything I want to share about CD because he's one of the few people I know that would make a "part two" if ever there was one.

He always brought playing cards for my oldest son, Aidan. When we had received over two thousand cards, I asked him to pause. He and his wife have blessed us in so many ways—food, generosity, support, networking, and, most of all, a genuine friendship.

But not every story has a happy ending. I became a realtor in 2022. CD was finishing his illustrious career in the military. He owned two homes and decided to sell one in Cali-fornia. I wasn't the most experienced agent, but I was very capable and will-ing. He said I would have the opportunity to sell his home, but he had one other realtor in mind. He called me one day out of the blue and said, "Make your selling pitch; now I have three realtors in mind, and I'll choose what works best for me." Long story short, we all made our pitch and he let me know he was moving in a different direction. I saluted the other realtor. I asked who was the lucky one? He said, "None of you, we're going in a different direction." It stung a lit-tle, but his call and honesty were clutch. I learned that it's important to manage your expectations. He's still my guy, and I believe he'll give me at least one real estate client for the amount of fire haircuts I gave him. But man, the Windy City is still a cold place.

HE AND HIS WIFE HAVE BLESSED US IN SO MANY WAYS.

Chapter 7

SIR WILLIAM
Please, Dad, Don't Shave Your Head

If you don't already know, I am bald. Actually, I am balding . . . ("Way more productive." —Isaac Witty.) I served in the Navy for six years. Most of us who join start with a full head of hair and are full of vigor. Few of us escape able to "keep that same energy." We age about twenty years and the receding hairline is obvious. Between the stress, energy drinks, and cigarettes, your average young adult looks like they're in their forties. The military was especially hard on my friends the Franks. I could write another book on the life of the Franks, Cece and Sir William, but let's just say, the military took their pound of flesh.

Sir William wrestled with the thought of losing his hair. He did NOT want to shave his head. He wrestled with the mirror daily and one day, in his distress, he consulted his barber. He said, "I saw a picture of my hair and it's time to let it go."

I replied, "There's no turning back if you do this, and right now isn't your time. If it was, I would have no problem telling you. I've had to do this a few times, it's not fun, but sometimes necessary."

He listened. But this conversation was ongoing for months, back and forth. I told him about my early days with the receding hairline and how I thought that trimming my entire head would help everything grow back evenly. *Lies!* Men, if you are not ready, do not throw in the towel. Use every resource, comb it over, use products, pray over it . . . *don't* get a man unit. By all means, *fight*. But Sir William was tired of fighting. Eventually, he threw in the towel and shaved his head. Cece didn't love it, but she loved him. He went for months with a bald head. He pulled off the look and enjoyed it. But none of us loved it.

MEN, IF YOU ARE NOT READY, DO NOT THROW IN THE TOWEL.

His five-year-old son was our only hope. He came to him in tears and said, "Dad, I miss your hair. I don't like you being bald. Can you please get your hair back?" What could he do? Was his hair too far gone? No! There was hope! Amazingly, after a few months, his hair returned to its previous form.

I was happy for my friend, and I tried to give him the meanest drop fade with a hard part on his next haircut. He was one of the lucky ones; his hair came back. I love you, Sir William, but I told you not to cut your dang hair!

Chapter 8

POOKIE
One Loyal Guy

Before I would ever be included in a conversation about the "best barbers ever," I needed clients. I needed to get better. I worked hard to get better. When I wasn't that good, I had people like Pookie. He was faithful from the beginning. He said, "I have been looking for a barber for some time now, and you are my guy." He meant it. He frequently came back for haircuts, and he would bring his wife. I took forever cutting his hair, but we had a fun time talking about life and the future. He told me to promise that if I ever left that shop to let him know. He had lost barbers in the past. Sometimes they just disappear. One customer told me his barber was shot and killed two days after cutting his hair. He walked in looking for a trim and found tragic news.

Pookie and his wife were going through a really challenging time. Unfortunately, she had stepped out of the marriage, and they were headed for a divorce. He was so downcast, he lost a ton of weight, and his usual spunk was gone. Sometimes you're the barber and sometimes you're the therapist. Our once joyful meetings turned into heart-to-hearts and encouragement. Over time, he bounced back, and they ended on good terms. It was also my time to leave, but I remembered the promise. I was moving to a different shop; he went with me. His

SOMETIMES YOU'RE THE BARBER AND SOMETIMES YOU'RE THE THERAPIST.

haircuts took much longer, and our bond was on a whole new level. The fun was back, the joy was back, and so were we. He later informed me I had walked with him through some of the darkest times of his life. He told me how much hope our little sessions had given him. Over time, he met someone new. She really enjoyed how he looked, but even more so after our sessions. He made me a better barber and those dark times gave us new light.

Did You Know?

Early in Egypt, barbers were also known as priests. They would shave and trim away "entrances" for evil spirits. It was good to have a good barber.

Chapter 9

V

Adios, Amiga

My mental barber notes allowed me to categorize most people. One of my observations was that Latinos tended to be extremely detailed. In short, picky. I was okay with that because black folks can be that way, as well, and I had gotten used to it. V was one of my early clients. She said she would profess her undying loyalty if I took my time and did her hair right. She was up-front that she had lofty standards and was willing to be honest.

I tell you what, though, that first haircut went well, and when she said she would be back every two weeks, every two weeks it was. There were a select few people that came to my house for haircuts for one reason or another. During the Covid pandemic, this was the case. I was honored that she still maintained her two-week routine, even if it meant in my garage. V and I had gotten pretty close, and we unloaded a lot on each other. She knew that I was pretty established in my faith, and I knew that she was different from most ladies in the military, but none of this ever hindered our friendship.

WHEN SHE SAID SHE WOULD BE BACK EVERY TWO WEEKS, EVERY TWO WEEKS IT WAS.

Unfortunately, we had an expiration date. V would go on to separate from the military, but before she left, she gave me a very patriotic pocket knife. I don't think she knew that I was the most unpatriotic patriotic person ever at that time. I am a proud patriot now! She also wrote me a little letter. The letter is packed away somewhere. She shared that our time together helped her keep going. She said that the time had greatly improved her mental health, and they just may have saved her life.

? Did You Know?

The only major difference between a barber and a cosmetologist is the tools they are allowed to use. Barbers are tested by the state board on razors, while the cosmos are tested on waxing. Everything else, school- and testing-wise, is virtually the same.

Chapter 10

SKYDIVER
The Resurrected Marine

Skydiver walked into the barbershop wearing a neck brace. After the small talk, I cut to the chase. "Lay it on me, man—what happened?"

He gladly told me his tale. He was a Marine being discharged from the military and decided to go skydiving the day before his discharge. The parachute malfunctioned and he fell, landing on his back. He survived, despite some insane injuries. The Marines allowed him to stay in until his injuries were better, which was incredible. I never saw him again, but I wonder if he ever went skydiving again.

I asked my wife about skydiving in the future, and after this story . . . it was a resounding "NO!!"

> **I NEVER SAW HIM AGAIN, BUT I WONDER IF HE EVER WENT SKYDIVING AGAIN.**

?

Did You Know?

The first Wahl clippers were developed by Leo J. Wahl in 1909.

Chapter 11

BAMA

Black, Loud, and Back from the Dead

Y ou get some customers that you *swear* will be coming forever, but I only got Bama for one incredibly special season.

He wore his emotions on his sleeve, a very jovial and upbeat person. Bama was in the top five as far as personality. He was a six-foot-two, extremely muscular black man from New Orleans. After giving him his first haircut, he assured me he would be back every single time. And he was true to his word up until I left that barbershop. Bama was always generous, so much so that I gave him a mug for supporting our nonprofit organization called Into the Harvest.

He unknowingly encountered a mutual friend of ours, DW, while he was cursing like a sailor. Bama was going on this day about something and DW said, "Hey, you must know Keith since I see you're drinking from that mug." Now Bama was brought up the right way, so after he knew DW knew me, he sat up straight, cleaned up his language, and was a completely different man. This tickled me and DW. He figured, *Keith's a pretty well-mannered man. If I'm drinking from this mug, I should show respect.*

It was one of my days with Bama that inspired me to draft this book. One day on the base, news spread about a chief select who had suddenly passed, leaving behind a wife and two small children. The people who came into the barbershop that day were aware of the news. I tried to lighten the mood that day by making jokes, trying to do a good service, but it had affected me, too, even though I had never met the man.

When Bama walked in, he said, "What's up, bro?"

I said, "What's up, you look thin?"

Bama: "You look so sad. Did you hear about what happened?"

Me: "What?" I was thinking he was speaking about the Chief select that passed.

Bama: "Man, I almost died last week, hence why I'm so skinny." He went on to tell me how he had a stroke and fell face down at his house, how his brother found him and rushed him to the hospital where he stayed for a week.

It hit me hard. I was thankful my new friend was still alive, but after the rough news about the chief select earlier, it was overwhelming. As tears streamed down my face, I told him I would be right back. I grabbed my phone and called my wife and kids to tell them all how I loved them and how grateful I was for them. I cannot say I apply this every day, but I have learned not to take things for granted, especially not life itself because it's so precious.

On a lighter note, Bama goes down as the pope of my meticulous customers and I still give him a hard time for it to this day.

I HAVE LEARNED NOT TO TAKE THINGS FOR GRANTED, ESPECIALLY NOT LIFE ITSELF.

Chapter 12

LIFESAVER

Chew Me Out, I Deserved It!

The first time I ever cut Litos's hair, I totally botched it, leaving a piece in the back extremely long. To my shock, he liked it so much he said he would come back. And that's exactly what he did. Tex became a very loyal client and a good friend. We often traded stories and motivated each other's goals.

TEX BECAME A VERY LOYAL CLIENT AND A GOOD FRIEND.

Some young guys from the church had gotten back into chess, which inadvertently got me back into it. I had never been a fan of gaming, but these guys turned me into one. I wouldn't say I became addicted, but I played when I could. Driving home one day, I was trying to finish a match I had started before I left work. The clock was ticking, and I was getting my butt whooped. I didn't want to toss in the towel and quit the game, so I continued as I drove. Obviously not smart. I swerved off the road, caught myself, and straightened out, but in the mess popped my tire.

I thought of all the people I knew in Imperial Beach who I could call to come and help me. Tex! I called him and fifteen minutes later he was there helping me change my tire. Man, our friend Junk chewed me out when he found out what happened, and I deserved it. But I am forever grateful for that day, knowing I had someone I could call for help. Thank you, man.

Chapter 13

THE HOGSTER

Helicopter Ride with the Hogster & Rihanna

Who came first—the Incredible Hulk or Hulk Hogan? My previous boss was a combination of both. He was very charismatic, a good leader, but abrasive and freakishly strong. An extremely outgoing and boisterous guy from Minnesota. We did not always have a good relationship. It was poor. He was a hard leader, and I was a poor sailor at the time. I was nineteen in a completely new country. Japan was amazing, but my brain was not fully developed, mixed with alcohol and some poor choices—*boom* goes the dynamite.

The Hogster and I had a healthy rivalry going. He was moving up in the military but didn't really have a voice with the young guys. I had a voice with the young guys and was moving on from the military. Sports was the common denominator of our connection. One time he asked for input from me to help lead the guys while he was giving me a ride home. Instead of taking the opportunity to give him tips, I finally had an opportunity to speak my mind. I cussed him out rather good and told him not to be such a jerk. This was bottled up for a while so it felt good to get it out, but I regretted that moment for the missed opportunity and what could have come from it. I was selfish. When the Navy was promoting the movie *Battleship*, the cast flew to Japan to do a conference on the carrier. Our mission was to safely fly Rihanna and the cast to the ship. Bakebezzy, my good friend, had a girlfriend who wasn't comfortable with him flying the ladies, so he let me take his place on the flight. The Hogster was scheduled on the flight as well. He had the helicopter with the ladies and my crew would fly the men. At the last minute, the Hogster got "Wanered." The flight commander changed the crew and somehow, we landed the ladies. (Yes, I legit flew in the back of a helicopter with RiRi herself.)

Years later I was cutting hair in the barbershop and saw the Hogster. I thought he looked the same, even better. Time had helped because our greeting was very warm. We caught up for a little bit and he said if he did not have a barber, he would come back. Well, I guess his barber had not given him what he wanted last time, and he was ready to venture out. I started cutting his hair. He got a high fade with a six guard on top.

We formed a new relationship as he became a regular. He had a lovely girlfriend, B, who had children. Like me, he was a stepfather, and he was doing a great job. I realized I could learn from the Hogster. Sure, we talked about sports here and there, but now we were talking about life. I designed my business card for real estate and barbering, I thought it would be neat to have him there. It featured him, a Navy barber who had to have the most Joe Navy sailor I knew. For some odd reason, I didn't tell him, but it came together in one of the most beautiful ways.

WE FORMED A NEW RELATIONSHIP AS HE BECAME A REGULAR.

This old boss of mine came to an open house I was hosting. It was a surprise; I was not expecting him and B. We had a fun time. He took one of the business cards and looked at the back. "Wait, that's me . . ."

"It sure is," I said. "I thought it would be cool to have you there. The next day, he retired from the Navy, and he told that story. He spoke very highly of me and my family, which was amazing. While in the service, he had to give a very honest, not-so-great report about my actions, and now he was standing in front of people, speaking highly of me. What a journey! I have a lot of love for the Hogster and we still keep in touch to this day.

Did You Know?

A barber in town will normally do about ten haircuts a day. At the Exchange, I once did fifty-seven. On a busy military base, thousands of haircuts are performed in a day. My hope was to balance quality and quantity.

Chapter 14

B-TRAIN
Doctor Trainore—First Cut, Worst Cut

My first haircut might have been my worst haircut. Poor B-Train! A brand-spanking-new Wahl clipper. An old mattress sheet because I did not have a cape. Limited tools with limited skills to attempt my first haircut. But I had watched a demonstration in school earlier that day and I felt like I was ready.

It began well—a good guideline and friendly conversation. Unfortunately, the rest was downhill. The conversation continued to go well, but the haircut . . . not so much. Three hours in, we both started worrying. The clippers were so hot I considered telling our roommate T-Dub, who was a firefighter, to stand by. Not only that, but with each mistake, B-Train's skin paid the price. So did my hand. He occasionally said, "Ow."

Finally, I caught on. "What's up, bro?"

He said, "They're really hot."

We discontinued the worst haircut ever.

He still let me cut his hair after that, although I do not understand why. B-Train was someone I had intentional conversations with during haircuts. There was a time in our lives where we were both growing as leaders, and Upstate New York and southside Chicago just did not mesh. Fortunately, he was an ex-Army guy. Those cats are tough. He took what I said to heart, and tried to incorporate it, whether fair or not. I loved him for that.

As my cuts got better, our conversations got better. It did not take us long to get into the "weeds"; the deep things came naturally. I looked forward to cutting his hair for the bonding time. Eventually, he became a solid tipper. (Clients can learn, too! Ha!) B-Train was there for every big moment: barber school, barber school graduation, my wedding, my first Bible study on base, my first open house, etc. He is one-of-one and no way I would be the barber I am without him. No way.

AS MY CUTS GOT BETTER, OUR CONVERSATIONS GOT BETTER.

?

Did You Know?

Andis used to make handheld clippers. In 1921, they made their way into the electric clipper industry.

Chapter 15

ZAY

Terrible Twos

This was the haircut that prepared me for children for the rest of my life. What a cool little guy Zay was! I liked him very much. We were on a ministry retreat to hang out with some friends in North Carolina, and while there, I befriended Zay, their son. He was two years old and had some developmental issues, but this made him even sweeter.

There is one thing I have learned about traveling with the trade—always bring your tools! At the end of the trip, his parents asked me the inevitable question: "Can you cut Zay's hair?"

How could I betray this little guy? What two-year-old likes getting a haircut?! Especially from someone they had liked. Past tense. He was not going to like me after this cut. The family had told me that this was one of his least favorite activities.

It was an all-hands effort. Zay has four sisters and a brother. I started combing Zay's hair as a tactic to get him used to me touching his head, but he knew what was coming. We tried to get done as quickly as possible. Zay protested strongly. His siblings gave him little bits of his favorite trail mix and took turns trying to make him laugh. And before you knew it, it was done!

But these were my people; I had to make sure everything was on point, so I said, "I just want to touch up a few more spots." Zay lost it. His dad, a godly man whom I admire as a soldier (and not just any soldier, but an elite Special Forces Army officer) grabs the little guy's head to try to keep it straight for this last little bit. Zay, at only two, was actually a valiant opponent for me and his dad combined.

Did I mention that this was the very first toddler haircut I had ever done? It gets worse. The family's begging Dad and Zay to relax. Neither was having it. I am cutting what I can, trying not to get distracted. But I was not an experienced barber at this point. I barely knew how to approach his hair. Suddenly, Zay choked on his snacks. The family panicked, but Dad was unaware because he was behind Zay. I was beside him with the loudest Walmart clippers in America. (Hence why I suggested bringing your own tools while traveling. My quiet magic clippers would have been clutch right then.) I legit prayed, *Lord, my cut cannot be so bad that I take this little man out. Please keep him us.* But Dad realized what was going on, cleared the offending snack from Zay's throat like a pro, and, boom, crisis averted.

ZAY, AT ONLY TWO, WAS ACTUALLY A VALIANT OPPONENT FOR ME AND HIS DAD COMBINED.

Zay eventually forgave me and played with me again. And his mom gave me the warmest, most genuine thank-you I have ever received after a haircut. After this, I was ready for any kid.

Chapter 16

MOMMA BEAR AND GOLDILOCKS

No One Else Will Cut His Hair

Sometimes words come back to bite you in the butt. Goldilocks was a three-year-old who was ready for action. I saw him playing outside the barbershop and I could tell he was going to give me a run for my money. Once it was his turn, Momma Bear said, "Let's see how he does." Unfortunately for me, she knew deep down what was coming; she just did not want me to know. I have never met a stronger three-year-old in my life. Goldilocks did *not* like hair on him *at all*, and even with the base's Shop-Vac, it was impossible to catch all the bits. He did not like the sound of the vacuum, he did not like the necktie preventing hair from falling down his back, he did not like the last line of defense—the cape. And he would not sit still.

But I am a determined person. I do not give up easily. I could almost hear Zay telling me, *you got this, bro, remember?* But I must admit, I was *not* ready for the guttural sound that came from this young man as I cut his hair. He belted out the loudest sound a little human could make, then proceeded to swing at his mom (but not me, which I thought was interesting). As people walked by the window, they looked at us with major concern. I looked at his mom, and she assured me it was okay to keep going. I saw in her eyes a helpless mom who just wanted her son to get a haircut. Determined even more, we got it done. She thanked me and gave me a solid tip. I wondered if I would ever see that little boy again.

Oh, I would! I greeted him with a smile and called him by name. But each time went like the first one. I would often warn waiting customers what was coming and that everything would be okay. One day we were talking about other barbers and past haircuts. Momma Bear said something to me that I will never forget. She said, "At this point, you are the only one willing to cut his hair." I believed her. I can honestly say it may not have been safe, but it was worth it to me. After I moved to my second location, other barbers successfully cut Goldilocks's hair, which brings me joy. I learned later that he had special needs.

In any profession, it is important to be kind and compassionate with others. Patience and understanding are necessary when working with those with special needs. Every time I see Goldilocks now, we greet each other with a smile.

IN ANY PROFESSION, IT IS IMPORTANT TO BE KIND AND COMPASSIONATE WITH OTHERS.

Chapter 17

SEVEN-FOOT WEDDING

Do you Mean the Whole Wedding Party?

Biggie was seven feet tall in shoes and Biggie was one of my longest-running customers. No one else touched his hair when I was his barber and I got love for him for that. On his wedding day, he and his wife, Bug, wanted everything to be right, so I was going to do my best to make the groomsmen handsome. What I did not know was that Biggie was going to have me cut the entire wedding party's hair!

Luckily, they were all the homies—White Magic, KG, Smackdaddy, and Griefs—and it was a blast. White Magic was the youngest-looking forty-something-year-old I had ever seen. At that time, he was doing a two fade and a hard part. His hair was very thick, stubborn, and black. Not a single gray. Giving his daughter away was a huge deal for him, and he had to look the part. Mission accomplished! KG was the cool dude. Unlike his two younger brothers, his hair was black. His hair came out *so good* that his date for the wedding would later become his wife and the mother of his children. Smackdaddy was the most handsome of them all. His cowlicks were fierce, but they were no match for a decent barber. Griefs was the wildcard—weird, fun-loving,

HIS COWLICKS WERE FIERCE, BUT THEY WERE NO MATCH FOR A DECENT BARBER.

and totally awesome. He had been growing his hair for a year with no trim, but for his only sister, he was willing to part with his gorgeous locks. Truthfully, I cut it too short. He was the last to go and the most challenging. I was tired and they can't all be good, right? He let me know it worked but was not my best. I appreciated his honesty. With the twenty pounds of hair gone, he danced like a madman at the wedding.

Griefs was also meticulous, but I appreciated that about him. He is very bright, like dang-near-a-genius bright. But the California school system got to him. He was not interested in college. After working at Walgreens for six months, he said he should have listened to his parents and gone to college. We continued the haircut as we almost died laughing. It was one of the coolest I-told-you-so moments ever. Biggie's wedding was amazing, and Bug was one happy bride.

Chapter 18

GUAM
Man's Best Friend

It is amazing the number of scars you can find during a haircut. I once tapped the back of my friend JT's head. He responded in a manner that I had never heard from him and said, "please don't do that." I thought he was joking until he pressed me. He said, "when you do that, it takes me back to a dark place where I dealt with abuse. I never did it again. I had unintentionally uncovered a scar. I had hoped this would be the last time. Or so I thought!

I only cut this young man's hair once. Guam seemed very upbeat, which I appreciated. Not everyone is, so you learn to appreciate trivial things. Who would have known that five months prior he had tried to take his life and was saved by his dog? He had been battling some very dark things only military folks can truly relate to and had plotted out his death. He had even gone as far as to say his goodbyes. Letters written and given to loved ones, but not in enough time to intervene. When he had an opportunity, he loaded his gun, went into his room, and prepared to pull the trigger. But his dog Bluey had followed him into the room, and he knew something was up, so he began barking loudly, crying and whimpering. When Bluey pulled on his leg, Guam broke down in tears and realized he needed help. Guam reached out to the military and asked for help.

WHEN BLUEY PULLED ON HIS LEG, GUAM BROKE DOWN IN TEARS AND REALIZED HE NEEDED HELP.

He told the story with no shame. It was encouraging that I was able to pull it out of him so quickly. He could use his darkest hour to reach and help others since he was willing to open-up and share. I thanked him for still being with us.

If you know someone who is struggling, please reach out and try to help. Life is so precious, scars can heal.

Did you know? In the Bible, God told Ezekiel to use a razor as a barber would to cut his hair. He compared it to a sword.

Chapter 19

BABY C
A Rainbow Baby

Everything started off normal with one of my clients. But one day he opened up to me about not being able to have kids. He and his wife had tried for ten years, to no avail. At the same time, my manager was going through the same thing. I had no idea how common miscarriages are; they had suffered more than one. I also had no idea that a rainbow baby was a miraculous baby born after a miscarriage. I was thirty years old when I had my first child, so I know what it feels like to not have kids and wonder if you ever will. He did not lose hope, neither did his wife. Their day would eventually come. Seeing this man light up from head to toe when telling me the news that his wife was pregnant is something I will remember forever. Months later, Baby C was born.

THEIR DAY WOULD EVENTUALLY COME.

?

Did You Know?

The barber pole was a result of barber surgeons hanging out their rags to dry. The white rags were stained with red from performing surgeries.

Chapter 20

FATHER-IN-LAW

*Dad, Papa Ron, Grand
PiPaPeezy, Good Ole Ron*

He was not too excited when his daughter told him she was dating again. Our first Thanksgiving dinner together was cool, but slightly awkward. He respected that I served in the military but didn't like that I knew nothing at all about fishing. He was, however, intrigued when he found out I was a barber. His previous barber was in jail, and he had been cutting his own hair. Vacancy, a spot was open.

I cut his hair faithfully. He was quiet, but precise. This contributed to my growth because I had to invest in high-quality tools. This was the reason he was okay with me eventually marrying his daughter.

I appreciate my father-in-law because he allowed his grandson, Aidan, to cut his hair. That was Aidan's first haircut, and he did well. Aidan learned firsthand how much of a servant you are as a barber and how a client can "get over your nerves," as Avery would say. My future prodigy J-Man also got his first swing at hair thanks to my father-in-law. I learned from him; that man could do anything. He battled addictions throughout his life, but at some point, he was done. I am honored to say he has been clean for over twenty years. I love that grumpy, sober man.

THIS WAS THE REASON HE WAS OKAY WITH ME EVENTUALLY MARRYING HIS DAUGHTER.

Chapter 21

BLACK BUDS STUDENTS

The Taint of Steroids

Navy SEALs are the tip of the spear when it comes to the United States military. They are the elite of the elite. They are warriors, whether sea, air, or land, and they get it done. Frogman! Michael Anthony Monsoor. Lone Survivor. Jocko. Goggins. Being in a naval facility, I sometimes got some pretty special clients.

Two students in BUDS—Basic Underwater Demolition Training, the toughest training in the world—came in, think about Hell Week, little sleep, little food, hours upon hours of brutal beatings. Thousands go through monthly, but few make it to the end. They were black. Not too many brothers go through or complete it. But in my eyes, they had everything necessary to make it through. What could stop them?

IN MY EYES, THEY HAD EVERYTHING NECESSARY TO MAKE IT THROUGH. WHAT COULD STOP THEM?

Steroids. Their whole class was performing above average, which the history and data of the program questioned. Questions led to suspicion, suspicion led to tests, tests led to accusations. Twelve members from their class were accused of and suspended for use of roids. Even if it was not true, this was a blow to that class. Good men let their dream of becoming a Navy SEAL die.

But not my two! As they told me their story, I was flabbergasted. How could this happen? I proceeded to give them haircuts like they never had before, as they told me a story I had not heard before. It took a year of fighting the case before an admiral got involved. They won the case, and it was back to the hell of BUDS. Last time I checked in, they were in CQT and should graduate soon. Exhausted but pursuing.

?

Did You Know?

Seventy percent of the Navy Exchange's proceeds go to the MWR (Morale, Welfare and Recreation) programs.

Chapter 22

BUCK

My Little Brother

Just a little nervousness. It was time for my wedding. And of course, I was cutting hair. My younger brother, Buck, needed a haircut. Now you must understand I was not always a barber, nor did I have any inclination to be one. So even though we grew up together, Buck never knew me as a barber. Military barbers are stereotyped as not particularly good. Which is true. Just being honest. Buck was okay with me cutting his hair until he got in the chair. Legit, you could see the anxiety on his face. He was almost sweating. He said, "Whatever you do, please don't touch my top."

BUCK WAS OKAY WITH ME CUTTING HIS HAIR UNTIL HE GOT IN THE CHAIR.

I put in my guidelines and framed the haircut, but he checked in the mirror at least five times each section. My future wife and kids happened to be there, and we were all laughing because he was a nervous wreck. I was like, "Bro, I am your brother and I'm also a licensed barber. You will be fine; relax." This went on for the next forty-five minutes and, much to my amusement, Buck did not stop checking, stop looking, stop verifying.

Then came the moment.

"Bro, the top of your head needs a little trim now."

"You can't touch the top of my head."

"Bro, just trust me."

"Nah, don't touch it."

Unfortunately for him, I am the big brother. I started trimming the top of his head. He held very still because he did not want me to mess it up. When the first bundle of hair fell on his chest, his eyes bulged. We laughed hysterically while I assured him everything was going to be fine. Finally, I stopped letting him look at the haircut because he was throwing me off my game and I wanted it to be a surprise. When I finished, I turned him around and to his relief, it was a solid haircut. He admitted he had been a little nervous, which we already knew, but it was still funny to hear him say it aloud. Little bro looked fresh for the wedding.

Chapter 23

UNCLE MIAH
New Hair, New Start

Uncle Miah was my first lineup, and lineups are extremely important to Black folks. If you do not know, just ask around or watch videos. I would say it is more serious than the pair of shoes you wear in the black community. Uncle Miah was one of my most loyal and regular customers during barber school. He made me better.

Uncle Miah was sixteen when I met him. He always rocked a sponge mid-afro. It looked surprisingly good on him, but I always told him to cut it short so I could see what it looked like. I waited about eight years for this moment. As many people know, when you go through a tough time or breakup, you often take it out on your hair. My boy went through an extremely difficult breakup, and he finally agreed to let me cut the top of his head. It took about an hour and a half, but I delivered one of the most amazing transformations I have ever done on an individual. It was anticipation, years of waiting, it was the desire to see him in a different form, but goodness, it was on point. His reaction was priceless! He looked so amazing, we thought he was about to ask himself out. Confidence restored! Sometimes new hair will give you a clean start in life. He was with me from the beginning. I practiced his lineup before barber school and cut his hair until we left

SOMETIMES NEW HAIR WILL GIVE YOU A CLEAN START IN LIFE.

San Diego. In barber college, we legit did a coordinated dance as I clocked out for the last time. Objectively, it may have been the best clock-out at Bellus Academy. He is genuinely like a little brother to me.

Did You Know?

Barbers used to be surgeons! The father of modern surgery, Ambroise Pare, was also a barber.

Chapter 24

DWEED, BAILEY, AND NATE-DAWG

I Got the Brothers-in-Law Trio

At various times, I cut three different brothers-in-law's hair. All top-notch dudes. Dweed, Bailey and Nate-Dawg are some of the greatest men I have ever met. We had some good times during haircuts. All generous in their own way, they each enhanced my life and barber career differently.

Dweed gave me the highest compliment a barber can receive: "This may be one of the best haircuts I have gotten on base. Wait, this just may be the *best cut ever.*" Dweed was also one of those rare clients that left a fifty-dollar tip. A legend. But pride before destruction, right? One day, I was on fire. There were about fifteen people waiting for haircuts, and most of them were waiting just for me. This can quickly go to a barber's head. Dweed walked in and gave me a look. My chair was the one for him. I assured him I could squeeze him in quickly. I was really into the haircut before his, but I was looking forward to a session with him. He walked straight to my coworker's chair. She was a fantastic barber, but I was not sure how to react. This was not a betrayal, but deep down, I did not know what to do. He came over after his haircut to see if I was down for coffee the next day. I really wanted to say no, but it is good to be humbled every now and then. Coffee the next day was, as the young ins say, lit.

IT IS GOOD TO BE HUMBLED EVERY NOW AND THEN.

Chapter 25

SALT AND PEPPER

Wow ... Just Wow

Salt and Pepper brought out the best in me. I do not know why. I just really enjoyed his hair. Salt and pepper got a tight fade and a mean edge-up. If there were any other additional services, he wanted them done.

My legacy began to grow in 2021. People were wanting to get a slot in on base and they sometimes waited for hours. This was unheard of on a military base. I had to be at my station and set up by eight a.m. I would sometimes get to work a little early.

One day upon pulling into work, my supervisor greeted me and said, "Hello, question for you. There is a guy that's been sitting outside since seven something this morning. You know what he wants?" I looked outside, and there was Salt and Pepper—coffee in hand, comfy in a lawn chair that he brought with him, laptop plugged in. She could not believe it. When it was time to open the door, she stuck around to see how this ended. Sure enough, he packed up all his belongings and came straight to my chair. She did not say a word, just gave me the "Wow . . . just wow" face.

> **I LOOKED OUTSIDE, AND THERE WAS SALT AND PEPPER.**

Chapter 26

LIL PAT

Maybe Next Time, Maybe Not

Not all stories have to be meaningful, important, or impactful. Some are just funny.

I met Lil Pat as a younger dude, about fifteen or sixteen. And we instantly connected. As young boys do, he was trying to grow a mustache, which I told him I could line up. As you can imagine, this area of hair is in a very delicate place. For some people, they have no issues, others are ticklish like a three-year-old. Lil

LIL PAT AGREED TO LET ME TRIM HIS MUSTACHE, BUT THERE WAS A PROBLEM.

Pat agreed to let me trim his mustache, but there was a problem. As my trimmer buzzed close to his lip, we locked eyes, and we started laughing. His lip was quivering like, "Save me before the trimmer gets me!" I tried three more times, but I could not even get the trimmer close to his face. Lil Pat said maybe if I surprised him someday it would work better.

I assessed that theory on the next haircut and went for it, but by the time the trimmer touched the bottom of his upper lip, he was laughing hysterically. I befriended his family, his grandmother, sister and uncle, they are amazing people.

But I was never able to trim his mustache.

Chapter 27

CHAIR

Unspoken Hair Profession Violation

Chair did the unthinkable. You could say a violation of the unspoken hair profession agreement.

He had heard stories about me before he ever sat in my chair. He was in the shop one day and I realized he was watching me cut hair. Sometimes this is normal; people are just interested in hair. But after minutes, he blurted out, "My name is Chair, and next time, I'm coming to you to get my haircut." He did not break the ice. He did not ask if I was Lakeith, the infamous barber. He did not ask any questions. He just announced he was coming to me next time, as the other barber is giving him a good haircut.

"Why," I asked. "Did you hear something about me? Good, I hope."

"Yes, my boy Doctor Trainore told me great things about you." This was fair. If Doc thought you were good at your job, he would invite the world. A masterful recruiter.

HE JUST ANNOUNCED HE WAS COMING TO ME NEXT TIME.

"I got you next time," I said. Sure enough, he came to me next time and I cut his hair. He painted me with the highest compliments a barber ever receives—that may have been the best haircut I've had on base, possibly ever.

We had a good time each time I cut his hair. Chair was one of those people who could cover a variety of topics and go deep at the same time. He was not only a good client but a good listener, and quickly became a good friend. He referred great people to me and talked me up each time. I hoped to do wonderful things with Chair someday, somehow, Lord willing.

He introduced me to Sunny. I was not too interested at first, but he said, "Just cut his hair."

?

Did You Know?

Aside from being surgeons, barbers were also specialists in teeth and nails.

Chapter 28

SUNNY

Black SAR Swimmers Represent!

S o, others may live." The motto for search and rescue swimmers. We were three generations of black rescue swimmers. Special forces jobs in the military are mostly occupied by white males. There is some variety, but in 2007, this was rare. There were about five of us tokens, and at my previous command, yet at this one, I was the only one. Token, like in *South Park*. It was mostly good times, though. Generation one.

WE WERE THREE GENERATIONS OF BLACK RESCUE SWIMMERS.

After three years, we finally received another black rescue swimmer—D. He had better hair than I. Bigger arms. More intelligent. Was he a better swimmer? We never got to settle that one. People I did not know kept coming up to me onboard the USS *George Washington* and congratulating me for finally not being the only black SAR (Search and Rescue) swimmer. I did not like him too much. Generation two.

But D profoundly changed my life. He gave me hope in faith again. (That is a story for another day.) I left HS-14 as the only black SAR Swimmer because D transferred ahead of me. Ten years later, to the day, I met Sunny. The only black SAR Swimmer at HSC-14 and he was full of hope. Generation three. Cutting his hair was a highlight of my career.

Chapter 29

AMERICAN NINJA WARRIOR

Anything for a Haircut

One of the dopest white guys I ever met, about twenty-one or twenty-two years old. He attended a Black church faithfully and had decided at an early age he would only let a brother cut his hair. He would let others, if *necessary*, but his preference was obvious. He was a handsome guy, often talking about ladies, could not wait to be a husband and a father. Truly a decent young man.

There was an active shooter drill, and the base was on lockdown. No one on, no one off. Our barbershop was a desert with tumbleweed blowing through. The main entrance was closed. The only entrance was through the door to the adjacent store. We figured no one was getting a haircut for the rest of the day.

Boy, was I wrong! American Ninja Warrior texted and asked if I was free for a haircut. The answer was usually yes, but not today. Too much craziness. But he would not take no for an answer.

So, I said, "This is what you have to do—climb on the roof, repel from the ceiling, take out the enemy, crawl under the laser, grab the precious jewel, and present the secret password to the guard." So, he did! Or, at least, that is what it seemed like when security told me later how he American-Ninja-Warrior-ed his way to becoming the only person to get a haircut during an active shooter drill.

My manager asked me what I had done to my clients to make them so faithful that they would come during an active shooter drill. Did this mean I was the greatest barber of all time? Word traveled quickly, and no one let me live down just how popular I had become.

HE AMERICAN-NINJA-WARRIOR-ED HIS WAY TO BECOMING THE ONLY PERSON TO GET A HAIRCUT DURING AN ACTIVE SHOOTER DRILL.

?

Did You Know?

Barbers used to perform something called enemas. Opt out of that one!

Chapter 30

"SHORT ACCOUNTS"

Definitely a Lifestyle

I worked alone for years in Imperial Beach, but when it was time for a change, I transferred from my base Exchange to the Coronado Exchange. I was now the new guy. A good amount of my clients from the previous base had come over, but no barber has a hundred percent retention rate. Still, I felt like mine was above average.

When a new barber shows up and already has clientele, this creates an opportunity for jealousy. I understand this. I see some haircuts and I am like, *Dang, that's so good! I could not do that on my best day.* Every barber has a run-in with coworkers, managers, or customers at some point. I tried to always be kind and make friends, but it did not always work. Barbers can be extremely dramatic.

> **WHEN A NEW BARBER SHOWS UP AND ALREADY HAS CLIENTELE, THIS CREATES AN OPPORTUNITY FOR JEALOUSY.**

I have my quirks and I admit that I am not always likable.

Everyone worked hard at the new barbershop and the tips were amazing. One day I didn't receive a few of my tips because one of my coworkers wanted to "stick it to me." This was part of my income, and I had a family to support. Fortunately, my mentor taught me to keep "short accounts," meaning not to hold grudges long-term. I never told the coworker that I knew, but I forgave them.

My manager came to me one day and said, "I heard you received an insane tip yesterday!" My good friend Bailey had left seventy dollars on a twelve-dollar haircut. That man was a legend. When I remember the few tips, I did not receive, I think of my friend making the entire company talk about his "insane tip," and I'm glad I let it go. "Short accounts" is a lifestyle. Thanks, Bailey, thanks White Magic!

?

Did You Know?
In Rome, the barbershop was the spot for chillin' and gossipin'. Of course, not much has changed.

Chapter 31

RJ

Chief, Senior Chief, Master Chief

People will come into your life and make you better. RJ was one of them. As a chief, he walked in and said, "I'll give you a shot. If you do your best and take your time, I will take care of you." That he did! My skills were nowhere near the greatest-barber-of-all-time level. I was not even decent yet. I will be back. Thanks for taking your time." He continued to come back and coach me, and I continued to get better. He told me his regular barber was looking for him and wondered where he went. The regular was a local off-base barber and he was dang good. He had gone to school with my wife, and everyone talked him up, and rightfully so. But he charged three times what the base was charging, and RJ and I were starting to develop chemistry. Even though it took an hour on a base, which was not ideal, RJ said it was worth it, which gave me confidence and pushed me to compete with barbers outside of the base.

> **"IF YOU DO YOUR BEST AND TAKE YOUR TIME, I WILL TAKE CARE OF YOU."**

RJ planned to move to Guam to get ready for his retirement. As they say, God works in mysterious ways. He submitted his paperwork to his coworker, but his coworker did not send the paperwork up. Instead, he took orders back to the mainland and made the next rank, which no one anticipated—Senior Chief RJ.

By the time he came back to the shop, I was really cutting. Blessed hands meant; his hair was going to be blessed. We talked through life and everything else. He bounced between the regular and me, but this was dope because it meant I was at least putting out comparable work.

Crazy enough, RJ was not done. He made Master Chief shortly after that. He went from almost retiring, to achieving the highest enlisted rank possible. He was now my regular. I am quite sure he gave me every haircut then. The sea was calling, the Navy was moving him again. We only had a few more weeks left. Our receptionist was surprised that he consistently left forty to fifty dollars on a haircut that cost twelve dollars. He remained my most generous client, and the one most responsible for my growth and development.

?

Did You Know?

Barbering is one of the oldest professions. Paintings on tombs in Egypt show barbers cutting hair.

Chapter 32

DARSKIE
Country Lovin' Keith

Good ole Wisconsin! I always took way too long cutting Darskie's hair. No, he's not black, but he has some street cred. Two midwestern boys, we just had an enjoyable time. His wife Jas also started coming to his appointments. I have mentioned some spouses making the experience more challenging, but she was not one of them. She added to the experience. We talked about everything under the sun and encouraged each other. Darskie would wait until the absolute last minute to get his haircut, which is why it took so long. When the country was up in arms about Covid and the social unrest, he brought me a lot of peace. People were so emotional about everything that it was nice to have reasonable conversations about the times.

WHEN THE COUNTRY WAS UP IN ARMS ABOUT COVID AND THE SOCIAL UNREST, HE BROUGHT ME A LOT OF PEACE.

In barbershops, people debate sports, which is topic number one. Some talk through women and glory stories. We debated music. Who did it best? The song was "Hurt." Originally done by Nine Inch Nails, covered epically by Johnny Cash. I must admit, to have your song covered by Cash is an incredible feat. So, who did it best? Most people I asked said Cash, of course. I thought the original was the one. Perfect, eerie, emotional, powerful, and still rockish. To my amazement, Darskie agreed and was one of the few who thought the same thing. I love that country lovin' foo'.

Did You Know?

The first barber chair was developed in 1850 and even had the same footrest we use today.

Chapter 33

JAKE FROM STATE FARM

Brother from Another Mother

When I first saw Jake from State Farm, I just knew he was a SEAL. A real team guy, chin up, muscles everywhere, and, at his core, humble. He was not a team guy, but he was legit.

I first connected with his wife, Ky Ky, over football. She was looking forward to the halftime show featuring Justin Timberlake and I was going to be sharing my testimony instead of the halftime show. She was not happy about that, but by the end of it, we were all conversing and having a good time. Jake from State Farm found out I was a barber and said he would see me one day.

That man was not lying. He came to the heart of Chula Vista, what most would consider the hood, and found me to get his haircut. "Are you pretty good?" I answered his question with a story. You know how some people start out and they catch on really quick and they're really good at it? Well, I started off terribly. First, I crashed, then I crawled, then I stumbled, then I walked. His eyes lit up.

FIRST, I CRASHED, THEN I CRAWLED, THEN I STUMBLED, THEN I WALKED.

We survived the haircut, and it came out okay. If I am being honest, it came out subpar. He liked it, though, because he came back for seconds and more. I cut his hair exclusively until he transferred to Hawaii. He was always sending customers my way, and that helped because referrals were key. His wife, Ky Ky, used to rock an undercut, and eventually she let me cut her hair and even do designs. Jake from State farm is just as epic as the guy from the commercials. He is the type of guy that I could challenge to do anything. From the 75 hard challenges, to reading the bible in 90 days. He considers me to be a mentor to him, but in my eyes, he's a brother from another mother.

Chapter 34

E

Battle the Bottle

I had always admired haircuts—good ones, bad ones, and ones in between. E always had a sharp haircut. He cared about his appearance. Vain or not, that brother was fresh. As we got a little closer, I began to ask him to let me cut his hair. His response was always a gentle "no" because he had a good barber. As my skills improved, I gained the confidence to say I could outdo his barber. I do not normally poach clients from other barbers. But sometimes, you just *know*. Eventually there he was, sitting in my chair.

At this time, E was getting a high skin fade with the combover, a lineup, and a hard part, all of which he really enjoyed. I took my time and tried to deliver a solid haircut, and he really liked it. Needless to say, he was in the book, and he kept coming back.

My man was an athlete. He had played college baseball and could hoop his butt off. He was a Surface Rescue Swimmer in the Navy, until he leveled up, and he made it through Special Boat Training and became a SWCC at thirty-two years old. Even being an older guy, he was still top of all his classes by the numbers. I would say he is a better hooper than I am, but I don't know—he'll have to play me one-on-one to prove it.

With great power comes great responsibility, and even greater struggles. He battled addiction badly. It got so bad his wife considered moving on.

I got a message from our good friend Rik. "Hey. E's in the hospital with a concussion and bleeding brain. He's stable, but we won't be around for a while."

He was dying and there was nothing I could do. I closed the barbershop, went into the backroom, and bawled my eyes out. He was so young, had so much promise, and I had to find out through a text. I was thinking, *I hope his wife is hanging in there. Goodness this is horrible. Let me read that text again. This can't be happening. Did I read it wrong? Brain bleeding. He will not be around for a while . . . Who? What?*

He did not die; he was stable. And the message did not say *he* will not be around for a while. Once I calmed down, I contacted his wife. He was going to pull through, but something had to give. He had to battle the bottle. He did, and to the best of my knowledge, to this day he is sober. I did embarrassingly admit to him that I mourned his death. In a way, I did because the old E was gone. But I hope this new one sticks around for a long time.

I CLOSED THE BARBERSHOP, WENT INTO THE BACKROOM, AND BAWLED MY EYES OUT.

Chapter 35

J-MAN
The Best Future Barber

His chapter as a barber is not even written yet. How will it be? Will he soon carry the torch as barber? Time will only tell. J-Man was a young man from North Carolina who was struggling in the military. No one tells you just how difficult the military can be sometimes. I hit my highest highs and some of my lowest lows in the serivce. He was going through one of those lows. I approached him as he ate and asked if he wanted to check out our Bible study on base. He said yes, but not today. At the same time, his grandmother, Em, was praying that he would find a community in the Golden State. He kept his word and came out to our study. We had a common interest in sports and hair. He had a Black barber who was getting his hair perfect. It was an expensive cut, but he was committed. He was also attending a local church.

Much to my surprise, he wanted to give me a shot as a barber. Over time, I became his barber and his friend. He started to attend our house church and was at our home more than my children. (I am exaggerating, but you get the idea.) J-Man was a cook in the military. One of the *toughest* jobs for so many reasons. I learned that as a barber your service to the client goes well beyond the chair. Without going into detail, J-Man

AS A BARBER YOUR SERVICE TO THE CLIENT GOES WELL BEYOND THE CHAIR.

was experiencing an extreme low. He was not sure if he wanted to continue with life.

His father Big Man said, "We have no one else; I am counting on you to help my boy. You are the only contact we have in San Diego." I was in constant communication with Big Man and Momma Bear. The pressure was immense, and I was not sure I was going to be able to help. But God brought J-Man through the storm, and he was stronger than ever. Now I am counting on him. "Each one, teach one." I am hoping that he carries the torch and becomes the best barber ever.

Chapter 36

CAP

Walking and Talking

Where should I start with the ole Captain?! He is one of my closest friends, but it didn't start that way. Before my time, Cap had a barber to whom he was most loyal. I like to think I am extremely personal, but from what I heard about the barber before me, I could not hold a candle to him. He had so many clients and he was the Man—funny, kind, God-fearing, black, and smooth. But that barber had a bad run-in with the company, things went south, and he was no longer an employee of the Exchange. This meant I not only replaced the best barber in town, but I was also the guy who took his job. Would my tenure end as his did?

HE IS ONE OF MY CLOSEST FRIENDS, BUT IT DIDN'T START THAT WAY.

It was not easy winning customers over. Additionally, I did not have experience. Cap was one of my earliest returning clients, and he chose to stick with me. This gave me tremendous confidence and I needed that.

Now Cap was not an easy egg to crack. He had walls up and for good reason. We had a good, intimate friendship inside the shop, but outside of the barbershop . . . nothing. I pestered him for a year to no avail, until one day, fortunately, I found an opening. He was telling me about his friend he walked with sometimes, just a suitable time for catching up. When I had enough details to make a request, I asked, "Can I join you for one of those walks, playa?" "Maybe," he said. Fast forward a month or so and you will find us walking together for the first time at six a.m. It was a good walk, unique; we learned about each other. The reason it is important to build relationships with people outside of the barbershop is because you never know when you are going to need each other.

For example, Cap was blindsided by the breakup with his longtime girlfriend. I do not usually go into detail about people's relationships, so here's a brief overview. She was a Christian who left him for one of the pastors of the church. Cap was a devoted Catholic and his faith meant a lot to him. The situation shook up his faith quite a bit, making it harder to continue seeking God and doing his best to live for him. But with help, talks, and a lot of walks, he overcame that situation. Cap is still healing, but he is not where he was.

Our friendship is deeper than ever. He is an honorary grandfather to my children. When I have real estate transactions in California, instead of booking a hotel room, I stay with Cap. When his old barber got his act together and began cutting hair again, he reached out to the captain, but Cap, after much consideration, said "Thanks but no thanks, I have my barber now."

Chapter 37

BEN-JAMMIN, MRS. MIC DROP, AND UNCLE LEVI

Full of Ideas

A haircut can go beyond the barbershop, as I hope you have seen thus far. Ben-Jammin, his wife Mrs. Mic Drop, and their oldest son Uncle Levi, the coolest little man, were one of those families who believed in me early on. My first shop in Cali was, as you know now, in the hood. This was no obstacle for my friends. I gave Ben-Jammin and his boy a two-hour haircut because I was still slow as a tax return in those days. They stuck with me, though, over the years.

The family bought a home in this amazing California neighborhood and their prayer was that someone from our community would do the same. Ben-Jammin was another Army guy and ended up in the Reserves. He made it into the Warrant Officer Program and was going to go to Georgia for training. They had purchased the home recently and wanted it to meet the needs of our church community. After a lengthy conversation, he asked if we wanted to stay there for a "discount." I was extremely grateful, but declined because we were under a lease. Then Covid happened. Ben-Jammin was delayed for months, during which time we finished our lease and switched to month-to-month. I swallowed my pride, went back to Ben-Jammin, and asked if his offer was still on the table. The answer was yes. Mrs. Mic Drop and Ben-Jammin allowed my family and me to stay in their house rent-free for ten months. This enabled us to buy our first home two houses down from them. I have been blessed by many generous things in my lifetime, but this tops the list. Our friend Matt was the loan officer that helped us close the deal. We had no realtor, so he helped both sides come together for a direct sell. Seeing this process and what Matt earned inspired me to get my license. Eventually, after several failed tests, I became a realtor. Ben-Jammin and Mrs. Mic Drop had another idea—let us get our friend Keith (the brand-spanking-new realtor) to sell an $800,000 home. God help us, that house was two doors down from mine.

Well, I did sell that home. It was madness. Madness, I tell you! But I had help with this deal. The other buyer's agent was solid but fierce, and she did not go easy on me for my first deal. I have nothing bad to say about her, only mad respect. The folks at Rieder Team certainly helped me out, but I kid you not, headaches. The new family was a blended family of nine, moving from Long Beach. They loved the home, came in above the asking price, and asked for concessions. They were first time homebuyers, but it felt like they wanted a Brinks truck for backup. Between them and their agent, my head was spinning. Ben-Jammin and Mrs. Mic Drop, thankfully, had total confidence in me, but when things became difficult during the transaction, they reminded me that the Long Beach family were going to be our neighbors, so if I didn't think it was worth it, I should call off the deal and put it back on the market. I would be lying if I said I was not tempted to put it back on the market, but I prayed on it. We closed the deal.

I was a little worried about our new neighbors. Would they like us? Are they nice? Did I just make a huge mistake? We were all cordial; we would wave and say hello each time we saw them.

Shortly after this, I got a call from the other agent. I panicked. Do they hate the house? Did they find something majorly wrong? Are they going to sue us? No, their fourteen-year-old daughter was diagnosed with terminal brain cancer. They did not have the heart to tell their new surrounding neighbors, so they asked their agent to reach out to us. When it felt like the right time, we stopped over there with flowers and a card. Kari allowed us to come in and meet Angel. The first thing she asked for after her diagnosis was her Bible. At this tender age, she was going to do her best to walk through this storm with God. On a high note, she got to meet Lauren Daigle through the Make-A-Wish foundation, which was special.

The next six months may have been the most unique months of our lives. The neighbors we had dreaded and worried about became some of our closest friends. We went to their children's birthday parties, graduation parties, and to everything else this traditional Mexican family invited us to. It was amazing! I even became their barber for a little while.

THE NEIGHBORS WE HAD DREADED AND WORRIED ABOUT BECAME SOME OF OUR CLOSEST FRIENDS.

Sadly, behind the scenes, we were planning our move to Texas. Our time in San Diego had ended, and, as much as we wanted to see everything through with Angel, it was time for us to go. We assured them that if something happened to Angel we would come back.

That something happened on October 5, 2023, at the tender age of fourteen. Angel was with God. We returned to San

Diego to be with our neighbors. The service was beautiful. When my wife and Kari saw each other, they held each other in a long embrace amidst tears. The only thing Kari could say was, "You came! You came!"

We love you, Angel, and we know we will see you again one day. Thank you, McKoys; you have forever changed and enriched so many lives.

Chapter 38

MORRIS AND JEANNIE

Tuesdays with Morris

Before we purchased our home, while staying at the home of Ben-Jammin and Mrs. Mic Drop, we met the Akers. Morris and Jeannie were an extremely sweet elderly couple who would be our neighbors for the next ten months. We hit it off almost immediately. We would BBQ for them; they would make food for us. We spent holidays together and attended neighborhood parties. They watched our three kids grow up and were some of the first folks to meet our newest baby.

An elderly lady in our neighborhood owned one of two connected houses; her son owned the other. She moved into a nursing home a couple of years prior, and her son kept her house running. She passed away not long after we moved on the street, at 102 years old. Her son decided to sell her house and put her home on the market. Our lovely neighbors spoke with the son and convinced him to consider selling that house to us. We became official Sage View owners thanks to that conversation.

I cut Morris's hair regularly and we somehow started the tradition of having Gentlemen Jack Daniels after each haircut while talking. He referred to these times as "Tuesdays with Morrie." I figured it was because we met on Tuesdays and his name was

Morris. It was not until later that I made the connection between his reference and the book *Tuesdays with Morrie*.

I cut his hair for the last time two days before he passed. We had been trying to get something in the books for a long time, but my schedule was insane. I could tell my old friend was growing impatient with me not being able to come over. He was not mean about it, but he *really* wanted me to cut his hair.

HE REFERRED TO THESE TIMES AS "TUESDAYS WITH MORRIE."

When I finally made it over there, he told me that he was worried about his wife and that he had been too hard on his stepdaughter. He felt down about it, and I did my best to encourage him. It was like he was making an apology through me. Morris was dying. He passed away just two days later.

His wife had us over to say goodbye one last time. We sat with her until they took his body. Hours of conversation and tears as he lay on the floor of the patio. He had a lovely service and people said wonderful things about him. His grandson reminisced about the first haircut Morris gave him. I found him afterwards and told him the story of me giving Morris his last haircut. Powerful stuff.

We formed a new friendship with his wife and daughter after Morris was gone. He had been the glue, but somehow, we held together. I think every man should have an older man in their life, to tell them stories and teach them lessons. I am grateful to have had Morris. He made me a better man, and a better barber.

Chapter 39

THE UNKNOWN SOLDIER

Don't Judge a Book . . .

One of my pet peeves is someone standing outside, leaning against the window, staring through the fishbowl glass. Staring into my soul as I cut hair. One day it felt like this guy had it out for me because he had this devilish grin on his face and kept glancing into the shop as I was cutting another client's hair. He did not look well either. For some reason, I was a little more irritated than normal that day, so before he came in, I played out a scenario in my head where I asked him, "What the heck are you staring at, man? You good, bro? Everything all right?" But I knew the Lord would not be happy about that, so I took a breath and greeted him as he came in. It ended up being one of the most meaningful haircuts I have ever done.

His appearance was different, his skin was almost yellowish, and he was very thin but always smiling. He was an E-9 in the Navy, which is significant. He was going on a trip to Australia to visit a friend from the past. Usually when guys tell me this, it is to see a girl, and it *was* a girl! But he wanted to see her "one last time." I asked him why and he told me he found out that he had Stage 4 cancer and the doctors had given him about four months to live. My heart sank. Here I had been so judgmental of this guy as he stood outside the glass. He seemed really happy and content, and I couldn't muster up the courage to talk to him about faith. He left and I felt I would never see him again.

Fast forward several months. I was standing outside the Subway on base. A guy came up to me wondering about a haircut. I had been dying for a break that day, so when I went to grab food, I was hoping to be left alone. As I ordered, he came over and stared at me as if he knew me. I had no idea who this gentleman was, but I told him I would eat quickly and that he could come over when I finished. Another pet peeve is when people seem desperate for a haircut without reason. Sometimes I get it, especially in the military, but *goodnight,* my man, why are you so thirsty for a haircut?!

Later in my chair, I asked him, "Do I know you?" I try never to be rude, but I grew up with nappy roots, so sometimes it just comes out. After small talk, I asked if we knew each other. He said, "I'm the guy who had cancer." My heart stopped. So many thoughts rushed through my head. I had no time to waste. After he caught me up and let me know he was doing okay, I cut straight to the chase. "You know Jesus? I genuinely thought I would never see you again, and I felt terrible that I did not ask you about faith." I cannot remember what he said exactly, but he identified as one of Jesus' men. I asked him if there was anything he needed, anything at all. He told me the Navy kept him active until he passed along and that his church had been providing for all his needs the entire time.

I lost it. This wave of emotion was something I had only experienced a few times in my life. Something about knowing he did not need me and that He had him covered reminded me of how small my part was in all this. I got to be a bystander for an incredible

I GOT TO BE A BYSTANDER FOR AN INCREDIBLE STORY.

story. I gathered myself and when the haircut was over, I gave him a hug and squeezed him too long. I could feel his fragile frame, but we both needed that hug. I never saw him again, but I know I will someday.

CONCLUSION

In two-way radio, there is the call "Lima and Charlie," which stands for the two letters "L" and "C" in the military phonetic alphabet. It means loud and clear! I want to make this part *loud and clear*.

I am *not* the best barber ever. I can name at least one hundred barbers who are better than I am. I have received so much praise for my abilities as a barber, but I am not oblivious to the truth. There is One who knows everything about your hair. Everything about you. The Good Book talks about no bird falling dead to the earth without his knowledge. He asks, "If I care so much about the birds, how much more do I care about people?" Then he makes a claim that not even the greatest barber of all time can make:

"Indeed, the very hairs of your head are all numbered. Do not fear; you are more valuable than many sparrows" (Luke 12:7).

Every hair on every head is numbered! So are our days on this earth. He is familiar with every strand on your head. My favorite moments as a barber came through someone who came to me as a referral. They would say, "A friend of mine told me about you, how good you were, and I just wanted to give you a chance for myself." That is my request for you! Give the best a chance, a shot! He knows you more than anyone ever will. His Son Jesus has extended an invitation, a way to God the Father through his work on the cross. He is always accepting new clients. We have a small window of opportunity to accept this amazing invitation as none of us knows when our time is up, so please, consider the Best.

ABOUT THE AUTHOR

Lakeith Jones is a proud Navy Veteran, born in Chicago, husband, and father of four. After his service, Lakeith went to barber college and got his license. He became a realtor and hopes to open a business in Texas.

Lakeith's Dream Haircut List:

1. Patrick Bet-David
2. Stephen Curry
3. Joe Rogan
4. KB or Ameen (HGA)
5. Jordan Peterson

www.ingramcontent.com/pod-product-compliance
Lightning Source LLC
Chambersburg PA
CBHW032049040426
42449CB00007B/1037